Men, Women and Children
in
Victorian Times

Peter Hepplewhite

WAYLAND

Published by Wayland in 2013
Copyright © Wayland 2013

Wayland
338 Euston Road
London NW1 3BH

Wayland
Level 17/207 Kent Street
Sydney, NSW 2000

British Library Cataloguing in Publication Data
Hepplewhite, Peter
  Men, women and children in Victorian times
  1. Great Britain - History - Victoria, 1837-1901 - Juvenile
    literature.
  2. Great Britain - Social conditions - 19th century - Juvenile
    literature.
  3. Great Britain - Social life and customs - 19th century -
    Juvenile literature.
  I. Title
  941'.081-dc22
  ISBN: 978 0 7502 6822 6

Printed in China

This paperback edition first published in 2012 by Wayland
Reprinted by Wayland in 2012

Wayland is a division of Hachette Children's Books, an Hachette UK Company.
www.hachette.co.uk

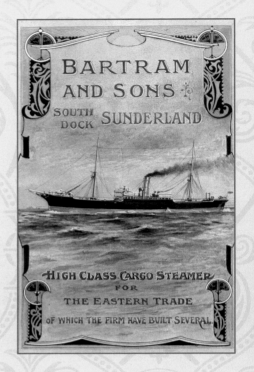

Picture acknowledgments: The Art Gallery Collection/Alamy: Cover (Main), 12; The British
Library/HIP/TopFoto.co.uk: 25; Mary Evans Picture Library: Cover (TL), 9, 27;
Mary Evans Picture Library/Alamy: 24B; General Photographic Agency/Getty Images: 13; The
Granger Collection/TopFoto.co.uk: 20; Frederick Daniel Hardy/The Bridgeman Art Library/Getty
Images: 8; Peter Hepplewhite: Cover (BL), 4-5, 21, 23, 24T; Lewis Wickes Hines/Corbis: Cover
(CL), 16; London Stereoscopic Agency/Hulton Archive: 15; Pictorial Press Ltd/Alamy: 10; The Print
Collector/Alamy: 11; © Royal Holloway and Bedford New College, Surrey, UK/Bridgeman Art
Library: 3, 22; William Bell Scott/The Bridgeman Art Library/Getty Images: 14; Shutterstock: 9,
Backgrounds; Amoret Tanner/Alamy: 26; Ian Thompson: 6; Wayland Archive: 18; After Franz
Winterhalter/The Bridgeman Art Library/Getty Images: 7

CONTENTS

Words that appear in **bold** can be found in the glossary on page 28.

WHO WERE THE VICTORIANS?

When Queen Victoria came to the throne in 1837, she was a young princess only 18 years old. Remarkably she reigned for the next 64 years until her death in 1901. Her passing shocked the country, as if everyone had lost a wise and much loved grandmother. Even before the Queen's death British people spoke with pride of living through the Victorian Age. In the study of history these years are still called Victorian times.

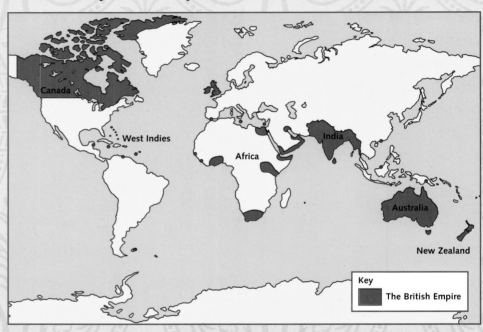

▲ This map shows the British Empire at the end of Queen Victoria's reign.

EMPIRE

The Victorian population grew from 27 million in 1841 to 37 million in 1901. And the numbers would have been far higher had it not been for the British **Empire**. By the end of Victoria's life Britain ruled lands that included a quarter of the earth's surface. Millions more Britons were encouraged to migrate and make a better life in countries such as Canada and Australia, which were colonies of the British Empire.

THE VICTORIAN TIMELINE

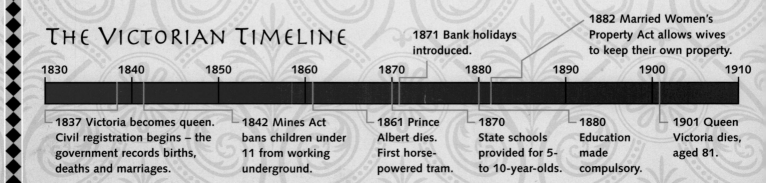

1871 Bank holidays introduced.

1882 Married Women's Property Act allows wives to keep their own property.

| 1830 | 1840 | 1850 | 1860 | 1870 | 1880 | 1890 | 1900 | 1910 |

1837 Victoria becomes queen. Civil registration begins – the government records births, deaths and marriages.

1842 Mines Act bans children under 11 from working underground.

1861 Prince Albert dies. First horse-powered tram.

1870 State schools provided for 5- to 10-year-olds.

1880 Education made compulsory.

1901 Queen Victoria dies, aged 81.

PEOPLE ON THE MOVE

To house the workers for these booming industries rows of narrow terraced houses spread across the countryside. Small towns such as Leeds, Manchester and Glasgow grew into teeming cities, causing a marked change in the population. In 1851 the **census** recorded that for the first time, anywhere in the world, there were more people living and working in towns than in the countryside.

A MODERN NATION

During Victoria's rule, life changed faster than ever before. Technology made Britain the first modern nation with a network of railway lines transforming the way everyone travelled. The telegraph brought fast electronic communications nationwide. By the 1850s Britain had become a mighty industrial nation, with mines, factories and workshops selling goods across the globe, from fine cotton cloth to steam engines.

REAL LIVES

PRINCE ALBERT

Prince Albert was the son of a German Duke. He married Queen Victoria in 1840 and they had nine children. Albert was interested in helping child workers and persuaded the Queen to support the great reformer, Lord Shaftesbury (see page 17). Albert was the driving force behind the Great Exhibition, the huge show in 1851 that celebrated British industry. When Albert died of **typhoid** in 1861 Victoria was heartbroken.

WHAT WAS LIFE LIKE IN A VICTORIAN FAMILY?

Most Victorian families, rich or poor, were larger than we are used to today. It was not unusual to have four or five brothers and sisters and for at least one of them to have died. As late as 1900, one in five children did not survive beyond their first birthday. Look in any Victorian cemetery today and you will find sad family graves with lists of children who died as infants.

HUSBANDS AND WIVES

In most Victorian homes the father was in charge and his word was rarely questioned. He was expected to provide for his family and earn enough money to pay the bills. A mother's place was in the home. Her job was to keep her husband content, manage the household and bring up the children.

▲ A Victorian family gathers to celebrate a baby's first birthday.

FEW RIGHTS FOR WOMEN

Women had few rights in Victorian families. Until 1882, when a woman married her possessions became her husband's property – even if she had worked for them or inherited them from her own family. Divorce was difficult, except for the very rich and it was considered shameful for a wife to leave her husband. Even if he had beaten her, the courts would not allow her to take the children or even see them without her husband's permission.

▲ Members of a wealthy middle-class family pose outside their house for a photograph. Mother and daughter have been playing tennis.

REAL LIVES

MRS BEETON

Mrs Beeton was not a typical Victorian woman. She helped her husband run a publishing business in London. She wrote a famous guide for housewives on 'household management'. It was published in 1861 and sold 60,000 copies in one year. The book was 1,112 pages long, contained 2,000 recipes and gave advice on everything from raising children to dressmaking and dealing with servants.

FAMILY HOMES

Richer, **middle-class** families lived in fine detached villas or terraces of large houses with gardens. Often these were in the **suburbs**, away from the smoke and dirt of industry. Most poorer, **working-class** people lived in terraces of houses in the town centres, near the factories where they worked. The houses were small inside and often cheaply built by greedy **property developers**.

In the 1700s and earlier, families often worked from home and shared a few large rooms with their servants and **apprentices**. During Victorian times as more people went to work in factories or offices, houses were built just to be homes. Rooms were designed for special purposes: a drawing room for receiving guests; a dining room for meals; a scullery for washing dishes – and in richer families a separate bedroom for each child.

▲ Slums in Victorian London drawn by Gustave Doré. The houses are tightly packed together under the arches of railway viaducts.

CHILDREN

Children of poorer families had quite a short childhood, often working long hours by the time they were 10. Many were **malnourished**, poorly clothed and so tired from working that the only day they could play outside was Sunday. Boys in richer families were sent to boarding schools at the age of seven, while girls stayed at home and learned skills such as needlework, to help them find suitable husbands. Almost all children would be beaten if they misbehaved.

▶ A wealthy family celebrates a child's birthday. Notice how much grander their party is than the one shown on page 8.

A WIFE AND MOTHER

Louise Creighton was a wealthy Victorian wife and mother who kept a diary in which she described her family life. Her husband was a successful churchman, who was to become the Bishop of London. Like many mothers at the time she believed children should be strictly disciplined. She wrote that, when her son Cuthbert played with fire, she held his finger to the hot bar on the grate 'so that he might feel how fire burnt'.

WHAT DID VICTORIAN MEN, WOMEN AND CHILDREN WEAR?

In poorer families, clothing was usually passed down within the family or bought from second-hand shops. Most garments were made from plain, hard wearing wool or cotton and mended until they were so worn they fell apart. If they were fortunate adults had one set of clothes for work and one smarter set for 'Sunday best'. Most poor people, though, did not have enough clothes.

THE WORST OFF

Families like the Colliers, who lived in London in the 1880s, were amongst the worst off. Mr Collier was a **blacksmith**. He had seven children and took their better clothes to the **pawn shop** at the start of each week. The boys had no underclothes or shoes, even in winter.

THE LATEST FASHIONS

Richer families spent a lot of money on clothes with the aim that what they wore would show their importance in life. Ladies followed fashion and eagerly read magazines like *The Young Ladies Journal* to keep up with the latest trends.

Early Victorian women wore full skirts with as many as six petticoats. In the 1850s **crinoline** skirts supported on wire cages were all the rage. By the 1870s dresses with a bustle – padding tied around the waist to make them stick out at the back – were very popular.

▲ This painting shows the plain clothes of an ordinary working family. The man is on strike and so is not earning any money.

Rich men wore knee-length **frock coats** made in silk or velvet. Underneath they had silk waistcoats, and shirts with detachable, stiffly starched, high collars.

HANDMADE AND SOMETIMES DANGEROUS

Until the sewing machine was invented by Isaac Singer in 1851, clothes were made by hand. Customers went to a tailor or a dressmaker and had clothes made to measure.

Victorian clothes could be hazardous. Many green dyes contained the poison arsenic. Sickness and even deaths from poisoned clothing became common.

▲ Victorian men and women pose in the sunshine for a photograph dressed in their best clothes. Most of the women are wearing hats and one is holding a parasol.

REAL LIVES

MOLLY HUGHES

Molly was a young wife in 1890s. As an old lady she wrote her autobiography. In it she recalled visiting her posh, clothes-conscious cousin in Guernsey:
'For breakfast she had a pretty flowered dressing gown. At ten she put on a simple costume for shopping. On returning she changed into a workaday dress for kitchen duties. For the afternoon a really good dress was put on for paying calls.' In all her cousin changed seven times a day.

What Jobs did Victorian men and women do?

By 1850 the Victorians could proudly boast that Britain was the 'workshop of the world'. A hundred years earlier most people had lived and worked in the countryside, just as their families had for generations. Since then a tide of new ideas and inventions had begun to sweep aside this traditional way of life.

▲ These iron workers are forging a piece of metal. Jobs like these meant long hours of hard physical work.

Industrial revolution

New wool and cotton mills, factories, iron works, chemical plants, mines and shipyards were built. Millions of jobs were created and people left low-paid work on farms for better wages in the towns. Historians call this the Industrial Revolution.

The census, a great survey of the population taken every ten years, tells us a lot about Victorian workers. In 1881 for example, just over eleven million were recorded, eight million men and three million women.

Jobs for men

Men did most of the heavy, industrial jobs. 760,000 were listed as metal workers, including 360,000 making iron and steel; 500,000 more men were miners and 270,000 were machine or tool makers. Almost 650,000 had professional jobs including 32,000 policemen, 23,000 doctors and 7,000 in a new hi-tech career – photography.

JOBS FOR WOMEN

There were more women than men in some kinds of work. Almost all domestic servants – 1,300,000 – were female, and many of them were girls under 15. Half a million women worked in the textile industry, most in cotton mills in Lancashire, while another 360,000 were **milliners**, dressmakers and **staymakers**. Some had professional jobs including 32,000 nurses and 13,000 teachers.

◀ Servants help a household of wealthy women to get dressed. The hoops worn by the woman in the foreground are to go underneath a crinoline dress.

REAL LIVES

THE BLICKS - A FAMILY IN THE INDUSTRIAL REVOLUTION

A government official's report from 1837 tells that in that year the Blick family lived in Princes Risborough in Buckinghamshire. Sam Blick, 41, was a farm labourer who earned 8 shillings a week (40p). His 19-year-old son William had no work. After moving to Stalybridge, near Manchester, Sam started work in a cotton mill, earning 12 shillings (60p) a week, while William got a job in a factory earning 11 shillings (55p). With the extra money the Blicks could afford to rent a cottage with four rooms and an oven.

WHAT JOBS DID VICTORIAN CHILDREN DO?

In early Victorian times children and young people made up a quarter of the workforce. In some cases this was nothing new. Farm children had always worked alongside their families. They started with simple, almost fun jobs, when they were little like scaring birds out of fields. Older boys worked like men, even handling teams of big horses pulling ploughs. Girls might work in the dairy, milking cows or making butter and cheese.

▲ This young girl is working in a mill in around 1880. There are no guards or grills to protect her from the moving machinery.

MILL CHILDREN

Almost all new industries used child workers. Bosses liked them because they could pay them less than adults and often their small size was useful for working in cramped spaces. Children as young as five worked as 'piecers' in the mill. They crawled underneath moving machinery to tie knots in broken threads. Sometimes they were pulled into moving machinery and horribly injured.

▲ A trapper boy holds a trap door open for a 'Putter'. Putters, like the man in this picture, pushed heavy trolleys of coal on small underground rail tracks.

MINING BOYS

Boys as young as six worked as 'trappers' in coal mines. They opened and closed trap doors to direct fresh air round the seams to clear explosive gases. Although the youngest and poorest paid workers, they were in charge of safety!

REFORM

In 1833 the social reformer Lord Shaftesbury persuaded Parliament to pass a **Factory Act** stopping children working in mills until they were nine. The 1842 Mines Act banned boys under 11 from working underground. Even so millions of children continued to work in other jobs, until 1880 when a new law made everyone go to school until they were 10.

REAL LIVES

JOSEPH TAYLOR, A 10-YEAR-OLD MINER IN NEWCASTLE

Joseph described his daily life in a government report of 1840. He said: 'I have been working about nine months and get paid 1 shilling and 3 pence (about 6p) a day. I get up at three o'clock in the morning and start work at four. I drive a coal wagon pulled by a horse. I work until four o'clock in the afternoon and sometimes get sleepy. Usually I fall off the wagon at least once a day. Luckily I've never been hurt.'

WHAT KIND OF SCHOOLS DID VICTORIAN CHILDREN ATTEND?

In Victorian times parents had to pay to send their children to school. The sons of rich families went to boarding schools like Winchester or Rugby, where they learnt Greek and Latin. Rich girls were taught at home. Boys from middle-class families went to fee-paying local grammar schools where they studied more practical subjects like science and mathematics.

▲ Pupils in Victorian schools sat in rows of dark, varnished wooden desks, all facing the teacher's desk.

STRICT SCHOOLROOMS

Victorian classrooms were quite forbidding. Children sat in rows of desks, sometimes in large rooms with several classes noisily side by side. The main lessons were the three Rs - Reading, wRiting and aRithmetic. Paper was expensive so younger children wrote on slates with thin slate pencils.

Teachers were very strict. Punishments included writing lines – copying the same sentence 50 or 100 times – or being made to wear the Dunce's Cap – a big hat with a capital D on it. Boys could be caned across their bottoms and girls on their hands or the back of their legs.

CHURCH AND CHARITY

Most children went to schools run by churches or charities. The National Society belonging to the Church of England was set up in 1811. By 1851 the Society ran 17,000 schools with a million pupils. In 1844 Lord Shaftesbury had founded the Ragged School Union to set up schools in slum areas of the new industrial towns.

NEW AND FREE

By the 1860s more than 2 million children still did not go to any kind of school, so at last the government stepped in. Locally elected School Boards were given money to build new schools. Even so it was not until 1891 that education became compulsory and free for children between five and ten years old.

REAL LIVES

MR MURRAY, A DEVOTED TEACHER

In 1847 the First Report of the Newcastle upon Tyne Ragged School described how James Murray took a job as Master in the new school. The school was in Sandgate, one of the poorest areas of Newcastle. Mr Murray soon won the affection of his pupils, as he was strict but kind. That winter, cholera struck. The deadly disease ripped through the city and many boys fell seriously ill. Bravely, Mr Murray visited them until he too caught cholera. Sadly he died leaving behind a widow and baby.

WHAT WAS IT LIKE TO LIVE IN A VICTORIAN CITY?

Early in Queen Victoria's reign if someone wanted to know what the future might look like, they visited boom cities like Manchester and Leeds. Here were the busy, dirty and crowded centres of industry that were transforming the nation.

CROWDED AND CRAMPED

In 1801 the population of Manchester was 75,000, but by 1851 this had soared to 303,000. Similarly Leeds grew from 30,000 to 101,000. Many people moved from the countryside for better wages, but they paid a heavy price as their health suffered. Workers lived in dense rows of small terraced houses, close to the factories where they were employed. These slums usually had few toilets, no drains and shared pumps for water. Houses were often lived in by several families, with perhaps five or six people living in each room. The streets were badly paved and full of rubbish, while factory chimneys belched out filthy smoke.

▼ Ragged and barefoot children play in the street in a London slum. The shops are selling second-hand clothes.

KILLER DISEASES

These conditions led to terrible outbreaks of infectious diseases like cholera and typhoid fever. In 1842 Edwin Chadwick published a famous report on the '**Sanitary** Conditions of the Labouring Population of Great Britain'. Shockingly, Chadwick claimed that people living in the countryside lived far longer than people in towns.

Victorian cities only improved slowly. Chadwick's work led to the first Public Health Act in 1848 giving local boards of health powers to improve the water supply and sewers in their areas. From the 1870s councils were allowed to pull down slums and build better quality homes.

REAL LIVES

ISABELLA HAZARD, THE 'BLUE GIRL'

Isabella Hazard lived in Sunderland in 1831. She was 12 years old and for the saddest of reasons was to become known as the 'blue girl'. Isabella was one of the first people to catch the contagious disease, cholera. Cholera is caught by drinking infected water and attacks the intestines, causing terrible diarrhoea, sickness and fever. The notes of Isabella's doctor report that she caught cholera on 16th October and died the next day. Her skin had turned a blue colour.

HOW DID VICTORIAN PEOPLE TRAVEL?

The first railway line predated the Victorian age. The Stockton to Darlington line was built by George Stephenson and opened in 1825. It mainly carried coal but once a day a horse-powered train carried passengers.

▲ This famous painting by William Firth shows the busy platforms in Paddington station, London around 1860.

TRANSFORMING TRAVEL

From this modest beginning came the explosion of railways that transformed the way people travelled. By 1845, 2,441 miles of railway had opened and 30 million passengers had been carried. By 1900, 18,700 miles were in use and over 1,100 million passengers had taken a railway journey.

Railways did not replace horse transport. Many long distance coaches went out of business, but more short journeys were needed to carry people around growing towns and to take them to railway stations. The first omnibuses – horse-drawn buses – were used in London in 1829, while the first hansom cab, a two-wheeled horse-powered taxi, appeared in 1834. Some horse buses ran on specially laid slotted tracks in the streets. They were called tramcars. The first horse trams in London ran in 1861.

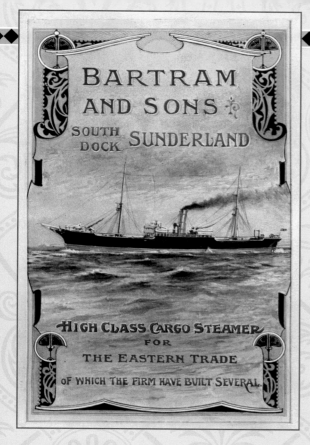

STEAM POWER AND ELECTRICITY

Soon steam powered trams appeared, only to be quickly replaced by the first electric trams taking their power from overhead wires or cables running between the tracks. By 1900 Britain had 200 tram systems, dramatically cutting the time it took people to get to work or school.

In early Victorian times steam ships remained an important way of travelling around the country. As late as 1849, only 6,000 passengers took the train between London and Edinburgh, while 12,000 travelled by sea.

◀ British shipyards such as Bartram's in Sunderland built most of the world's passenger and cargo ships in Victorian times.

REAL LIVES

TRAM DRIVER IN TROUBLE

Local newspapers in Blackburn reported how, on 7th August 1882, tram driver Mr W. Robinson was in a hurry. He worked for Blackburn trams and he was driving a football special. The crowds heading for the match were huge and against the rules he allowed the passengers to cram themselves aboard. Worse, he broke the 8mph speed limit, tearing down a hill at a breakneck 16mph. When he hit the curve at the bottom the tram overturned. One passenger was killed and seven were seriously injured.

How did people have fun in Victorian times?

Having fun became big business during Victorian times. This was the start of what we now call the leisure industry. Gradually working hours fell and wages went up. Many factories began to close for a week in the summer and in 1871 a new law gave everyone four Bank Holidays a year. By the 1880s most working people had time and money for entertainment.

▶ A Victorian postcard sent from a seaside resort. Railways and cheap train fares made holidays and day trips to the seaside possible for millions of Victorians. Hotels and lodging houses were built to accommodate tourists, while parks, piers and **promenades** were created to entertain them.

▲ This picture shows popular acts at a Victorian circus. The clowns are performing with horses and dogs while the ring master looks on.

CIRCUS FUN

Circuses and fairs toured the country offering family fun. They travelled in convoys of wagons and caravans towed by horses or steam traction engines. Acts included performing animals, 'freak shows' (such as 'the bearded lady') and **trapeze artists** who performed acrobatics high above admiring crowds.

MUSIC HALLS

Music halls were popular with adults as tickets only cost a few pennies and the venues sold alcohol too. By 1880 there were more than 500 halls in Britain playing to packed houses. Stage acts had catchy names so they would stand out on advertising posters, names such as *Professor Parker with his Highly Trained Dogs* and *Little Eric, the Australian Boy Comedian*.

▲ The Wardroper twins were a novelty music hall act who mimicked other, probably more famous acts.

SPORT FOR ALL

Many of the sports we enjoy today became popular in the Victorian times. The Football Association was set up in 1866 and lawn tennis began in 1874. The first Wimbledon men's championship was held in 1877 and the following year the first Australian cricket team toured England.

REAL LIVES

GEORGE LOCHART: ELEPHANT BOY

George was born into a circus family in 1887 and grew up to become an expert on performing elephants. His father ran a famous elephant show, so the family called their house in Brighton Elephanta Lodge. In his autobiography, George recalled how, as a toddler, he was sternly warned 'never get between an elephant and a wall'. This wise advice kept him safe and as a youngster he trained elephants to ride tricycles, play musical instruments and fire cannons.

How important was religion for the Victorians?

Many Victorians were Christians but even so they often disagreed about the best way to worship God. Most rich and middle-class families went to Church of England or Anglican services every Sunday. This was the official Church of the nation and it was very powerful. The Church of England ran most schools and its Bishops sat in the House of Lords helping to make laws.

Different Christians

Other families thought Church of England ministers and teachings were too self important. They joined other Christian groups such as the Methodists, Baptists and **Quakers**, worshipping in plain and simple chapels and meeting houses. During the 1840s a wave of Irish immigrants came to work on building projects such as the railways and their numbers boosted the Catholic faith.

Not going to church

In 1851 a census of church attendance uncovered a fact that shocked Christians of every kind: around 40 per cent of the population did not go to any kind of service on a Sunday. This meant that millions of families, especially those in city slums, knew little about Jesus and the Bible. And since they had no faith to help them, respectable Victorians believed this explained why many spent their wages drinking and behaving badly. Something urgent had to be done!

▲ A service takes place in a Victorian church decorated for Christmas.

Teaching about God

A great crusade began. New churches and chapels were built in the poorest areas and social clubs set up where families could find enjoyment away from the pub. Children could join the '**Band of Hope**' and take the pledge to never drink alcohol. Sunday schools offered the chance to learn to read and to learn Bible stories. To keep children coming back there were plenty of treats, perhaps a special tea, a picnic, an outing to the park or a boat trip.

"Saved"

◄ A poor family turn to God and are 'saved' in this picture showing the work of the Salvation Army. This was a Christian organisation founded by William Booth in 1865. The 'Sally Army' preached in the slums of the great cities.

ELIZABETH FRY

Elizabeth was born into a Quaker family, the daughter of a wealthy banker. In 1813 she visited Newgate Prison in London. She kept a journal in which she described her horror at the condition of the 300 women and children she found there. They slept on the floor without bedding and washed and cooked in the same grim wards. After this visit, Elizabeth spent her life campaigning to reform prison conditions. Queen Victoria took an interest in her work and met Elizabeth twice.

GLOSSARY

apprentices Young people who are learning a trade.

Band of Hope A Victorian religious club for working-class children. Members pledged never to drink alcohol.

blacksmith Someone who shapes iron into horseshoes and fits them to horses.

census A survey collecting information about the lives of everyone in the country. A detailed census has been taken every ten years since 1801.

crinoline A stiff petticoat that was worn to help a dress stand out in a bell shape.

Empire Lands governed by one country.

factory acts Laws to improve conditions for workers, especially children.

frock coat A coat worn by men that reached to the knees.

malnourished Badly fed, even half starved

middle class Families who are not poor and not especially rich.

milliner A hat maker

music hall A type of theatre, but with a variety of different acts shown on stage.

pawn shop A shop that lends money in return for objects of value. The objects are sold if the loan is not repaid.

promenade A paved public walkway along a seafront.

property developers Business men who buy land and build houses on it.

Quakers Members of the Society of Friends, a Christian group founded in the 17th century.

sanitary Clean, hygienic.

staymaker Corset makers, who made garments to help women look slim.

suburbs Areas of housing on the edge of a city.

trapeze artists Acrobats who perform on wires or ropes high in the air.

typhoid A killer disease with early symptoms that include fever, vomiting and stomach pains. Typhoid can be spread by infected food.

working class People who earned their living by working, for example in factories.

Further Information

More books to read

Nicola Barber
Victorian Life: Homes, School
and **Transport**
(Wayland 2008)

Liz Gogerly
Victorian Life: Clothes
(Wayland, 2008)

Peter Hepplewhite
A Victorian Journey
(Wayland, 2004)

Angela Royston
History from Objects: The
Victorians
(Wayland, 2010)

Richard Wood
The Daily Life of a Victorian
Street Seller
(Wayland, 2008)

Richard Wood
Look Inside: Victorian House
(Wayland, 2007)

Useful websites

www.bbc.co.uk/schools/primaryhistory/
victorian_britain
BBC website focusing on children in
Victorian Britain.

http://www.woodlands-
junior.kent.sch.uk/Homework/victorians
A brilliant school website with some great
information.

http://www.visionofbritain.org.uk/index.jsp
Vision of Britain is an astonishing site full of
facts and figures about Britain since 1801,
including lots about the census.

www.learningcurve.gov.uk/victorianbritain
Lots of material from the National Archives
written, drawn and photographed by the
Victorians themselves.

http://www.britishempire.co.uk/
Find out all you need to know about the
Empire at this website, written by teachers.

Places to visit

Black Country Living Museum
Tipton Rd, Dudley, DY1 4SQ
0121 557 9643
Don't miss the ride on the canal boat at this
open air museum.
http://www.bclm.co.uk/index.htm

Iron Bridge Gorge Industrial Museum,
Coach Road, Coalbrookdale,
Telford, TF8 7DQ
The birthplace of the Industrial Revolution.
www.ironbridge.org.uk/

Ragged School Museum
46-50 Copperfield Road, London, E3 4RR
Attend a Victorian lesson.
http://www.raggedschoolmuseum.org.uk/next
gen/

Big Pit: National Coal Museum
Blaenafon, Torfaen, NP4 9XP
A real coal mine to go down.
http://www.museumwales.ac.uk/en/bigpit/

Index

Numbers in **bold** indicate pictures.